*Crisis Leadership
The Navy Way*

CRISIS LEADERSHIP
THE NAVY WAY

Jim Hull

George Sauer

Copyright © 2010, 2021 by Jim Hull and George Sauer

All Rights Reserved. This book, or parts thereof, may not be reproduced in any form without permission.

Cover layout and book design by
Christopher Green Design
christophergreen.com

Back Cover Painting ISS at Mars *by*
Jim Hull
hullart.com

Printed in the United States of America
10 9 8 7 6 5 4 3 2

This book is dedicated, on the occasion of our 50th Reunion, to all of our classmates from the United States Naval Academy class of 1970.

In Memoriam

Charles D. (Chuck) Potter

James D. (Doug) Traver

Douglas W. (Doug) Dietz

Jay Jenkins

Members of the 9th Company, USNA '70

FOREWORD TO THE ORIGINAL EDITION

From time to time everyone faces crisis situations where new and more stringent limits are imposed on their best laid plans. We met in June of 1966, both reporting to the United States Naval Academy as Midshipman. From the time we reported to the Academy, until we left, we had to learn to deal with restricted limits. Many types of limits were placed on us. This required us to learn how to deal effectively and consistently with less than we had in civilian life.

At the Naval Academy, this indoctrination into the idea of limits began with Plebe Summer. Immediately, we had more to do in less time. Everything had to be delivered on time and with no excuses. For those of us who survived that summer it taught us to think differently in terms of resourcefulness. It caused us to begin to think differently in terms of what was possible. For most of us it forever changed our habits and view of the world. We learned that there is always a better way.

This new way of thinking helped us become more productive and learn to lead our way through situations where new and more stringent limits had been placed on us. We went on to apply these lessons as we pursued our careers and personal lives. To us this new way of thinking, and the process for dealing with crisis generated limits, had become the new 'way'.

When we got together at our 30th reunion in 2000 we began to talk about the changes at the Academy and the Navy in general. This led us to reflect on the lessons we had learned and our experiences over the years. We realized that, while not all our classmates had come away with the same lessons, the two of us had learned an effective process for dealing with, and leading through, crisis situations. The payoff, as we discovered, is that this process is even more powerful when used in non-crisis situations. It is with this book that we seek to share this process with you.

Jim Hull and George Sauer

June 2010

FOREWORD TO THE 10TH ANNIVERSARY EDITION

It has been 10 years since we penned our original book. In the interim years we continued to discuss leadership and its challenges. The biggest question we faced was whether a leader is born and/or can one be trained? In our opinion it is neither. Leadership is a chosen lifestyle. With that said the myth of the born leader, or the one trained, goes away to reveal that all along everyone that has ever been born has had the opportunity to lead. It is a choice. Why have most chosen to follow rather than lead? It is because once you choose a leadership lifestyle you make a commitment to make things better. No matter who you join, or what career you may pursue, in the course of your life you do it as a leader. You are committed to not accept the status quo but rather make things better.

We all know people who seem to quickly rise to the top in organizations they join. This is because they never accept the status quo. They seek to improve everything. Their point of view is that everything is subject to improvement. Everything is sub optimal. Therefore, they seek to make it better for themselves and everyone else involved.

In addition, the leader's lifestyle requires that they act with character displaying the highest values that demand respect and create trust. It is this commitment to make things better and the difficulty of living to high standards that drive most people to simply follow.

To follow is to accept the current state of affairs as good enough. It is to hope that nothing will change enough to force a response.

Followers operate within the given environment but do not seek to lead their organizations or groups to a better and more productive level of performance. They manage and administrate but do not lead. To lead is to always be moving and charging toward better and higher ground.

In the first edition of this book we offered a leader's way of thinking in the form of a limit driven process. It is a way to create solutions to problems associated with crisis situations. It is thus a bottom-up approach to making things better and providing an appropriate response.

We explored the concept of limits. These limits are the things that create the crisis. They are usually associated with resources. This bottom-up process provides a way to employ a leader's mindset one step at a time, situation by situation, and reaction to reaction. It is, however, but one way to lead people out of crises.

At the end of the first edition, in the chapters on leveraging limits and new opportunities, we hinted at what is now explored in more detail in this updated edition. Chapter Eight covers this top-down process.

Beyond the incremental model of building up from the bottom this new approach seeks to give the leader a point of view that is more strategic and global. It is a way to act that alleviates the need to react later. This top-down model is known as the Transformational Model.

This model seeks to transform the areas where the leader has chosen to focus their efforts and talents. It is the way a person who has chosen a leadership lifestyle thinks and acts. In this new edition we provide examples of how this mind set works and why it is important for anyone who has chosen the lifestyle of a leader.

In Chapter Nine we cover a process to successfully create a model for your own leadership lifestyle. Leadership lifestyles, while sharing some common attributes, are unique and must be tailored for each person. It is not easy to lead. You cannot lead part of the time. If the leadership lifestyle is chosen you must lead all the time. To choose to lead, therefore, is an act of courage.

A lot of people have led prosperous lives as followers. But given a choice the road to the leadership lifestyle is one that is not to be missed.

We hope that this new edition will inform and challenge more of you to pick up the leadership lifestyle. If chosen it can help you make this world a better place for the generations to come.

Jim Hull

George Sauer

50th Reunion Celebration, USNA Class of 1970

Contents

THE KENNEDY INCIDENT 1

THE LIMIT DRIVEN LEADERSHIP PROCESS.... 17

THE NAVSTA KEFLAVIK INCIDENT 39

THE ASHEVILLE INCIDENT................................... 51

LEVERAGING THE POWER OF LIMITS 65

THE APOLLO OPPORTUNITY 77

THE INTERNATIONAL SPACE STATION

OPPORTUNITY... 87

THE TRANSFORMATIONAL MODEL 99

THE LEADERSHIP LIFESTYLE 117

CONCLUSION... 125

AFTERWORD 131

INTRODUCTION TO LEADERSHIP

It is important to understand the common elements of a leadership lifestyle before proceeding to read about the special case of Crisis Leadership. Since the first edition of this book ten years ago, a clear definition of great leadership was provided by Forbes Magazine.

"A great leader possesses a clear vision, is courageous, has integrity, honesty, humility and clear focus. Great leaders help people realize their goals, are not afraid to hire people who are better than them and take pride in the accomplishments of those they lead along the way."

As a follow up to this definition we felt it was important to define each element so that a clear picture of a person leading a great leadership lifestyle can be attained. These elements form a Lifestyle Map.

The first element is a clear vision. What is a clear vision? A clear vision is a statement of a future state of affairs that can be easily understood by those being led. It is concise, succinct, and complete. It is easily remembered and embraces those things that are important, or should be important, to the people being led. It is not just the idea contained in the vision but also the clarity of how that idea is expressed by the leader.

The second element is courage. What is courage? Courage is the act of doing or saying what is right despite the consequences. Courageous people do not 'go along' with the pack, take the easy way out, or say what is expected. They are authentic. They say what in their heart is the right thing to be said and act in the same manner. They can be trusted to do the right thing in any circumstance. They know that the expedient is not what is in their, or their followers, best interest. They never give in to the idea that the end justifies the means.

The third element is integrity. What is integrity? The dictionary definition is, 'the quality of being honest, and having strong moral principles, moral uprightness.' Being honest means never lying and always being completely truthful. This last part is important because incomplete truth is a form of a lie. So, if you lie to mislead, or cover up, you are in essence morally bankrupt and corrupt. This also means that you cannot have partial integrity. You have it or you don't. In the end, as with courage, the person with integrity can be trusted.

The fourth element is honesty. We used this word to describe integrity but what does it mean to be an honest person? It means to speak the truth and to act truthfully. So then, what is truth? It is a fact or belief that is in accordance with reality. It is objective and not subjective. It is not conditional. It is what is! But it is what is today. It could change tomorrow based on new evidence. But it is evidential truth.

In society we have things and ideas that can be proven based on the use of our five senses. Then we have beliefs that cannot be proven but are none the less very real to those that abide by them. It is the former that we are referring to when we use honesty as a condition leading to a great leadership lifestyle. This also means that you cannot make something the truth by wishful thinking!

The fifth element is humility. What is humility and how do we recognize it? It is the modest point of view of one's own importance. It is not 'I' who stands at the middle of the universe but rather we or us. It is not the lowering of oneself or one's self esteem below that of others but rather considering and treating others on the same level as oneself. It is an attitude that my abilities do not make me better than you, just different. It is a point of view that sees everything as a vast connected network of relationships. It is not a hierarchical situation with me at the top as the leader and everyone else below me. Being humble allows me to treat everyone with respect and that leads to trust.

The sixth element is clear focus. In concert with the first element of clear vision, the great leader must possess clear focus. This allows the clear vision to be realized. Without focus and concentration on the achievement of the vision the followers will become confused and misdirected. All the actions taken by great leaders support a vision and make progress toward its achievement. This means that sometimes 'opportunities' arise, that do not fit the vision, and have to be ignored. If an opportunity does not support the vision the great leader must 'pass' on it or amend the vision in some way to include it. If this is not done the clarity of the vision is lost along with the momentum toward its realization.

Hiring the best and taking pride in their accomplishments is the way a leader defines his or her relationship to their followers. As a humble person the leader knows that they are not the most skilled or knowledgeable in all areas. They hire those that are better than them so they can weave together an organization that is strong on all fronts. They see the organization as an organic entity that will learn and grow. As such it needs to be motivated through encouragement and celebration of achievements by all members. This also breeds respect and trust.

In the end a great leader, with their Lifestyle Map, is a designer and orchestrator of an organization consisting of people, systems and processes focused on achieving a grand and purposeful vision. They are not feared but rather find themselves admired by their followers. This is the most powerful way to create a future and it is great leaders and their chosen lifestyle that take us there.

With this introduction to the common elements of a leadership lifestyle our book turns to address one special form of leadership. As the adage goes, 'we can make all the plans for the war but after the first engagement we have to innovate'. That is what this book addresses. What do we do, and how do we think, when challenges have become problems and problems have become crises?

INTRODUCTION TO THE BOOK

For our purpose in this book, crises are defined as an event or turning point leading to the need for decisive change. It is these small and large crises that are always getting in the way of a normal progression of events. It seems that no matter how hard you try life never goes quite as planned. Some people learn to successfully cope with this situation and others struggle. The purpose of this book is to provide an insight into succeeding in such circumstances. This insight is in the form of a process. As a process it can be learned and applied by anyone, in any walk of life who has chosen the Leadership Lifestyle. The goal of the process is to help you succeed each time you are challenged by a change to less-than-ideal circumstances. It is the way to lead to a new and better situation.

Where do Crisis come from? They come from a process. This process begins with a challenge. For instance, it is a challenge for all government bodies to provide and improve infrastructure. If they don't, the challenge will become a problem. A problem is created when leadership does not address a given area, such as infrastructure, at the challenge level. If leadership continues to ignore, or put off addressing a problem, it will at some point become a crisis. This means that leaders create problems by neglect and lack of personal accountability.

They cannot blame anyone, or anything, for crises as they are for the most part all self-created. Unfortunately, it is usually not until a problem becomes a crisis that leaders react. At the crisis point all power to 'act' is lost, and reaction is the only alternative.

As we are writing this new edition the world is experiencing a Pandemic Crisis. This crisis came from a problem, and the problem came from a challenge. The world knew all along what would happen if it did not fully prepare. But it did not. There is, however, another way. A path, not often taken, to allow us to alleviate crises. The first edition of this book ended with an overview of this pathway. Our new edition addresses this alternate pathway in more depth.

The contents of this book are an integration of the experiences and ideas from both of our careers. George Sauer graduated from the Naval Academy and pursued a career in the Navy. Jim Hull left the Naval Academy, after two years, and pursued a career as a business consultant. While we both pursued different life careers, we followed the leadership lessons learned at the Academy. This book is not intended to suggest that this is the way that the Navy always deals with crises. It is, however, a reflection on one of the best leadership lessons we learned. It was the lesson on how to deal with, or avoid, crises generated by restricted limits.

The best way to read this book is to proceed one chapter at a time. Each chapter builds on the previous one. This book provides an understanding and examples of the process and its two approaches.

The Navy stories reflect the application of that process and are from George's naval career. The specific process, and other concepts and stories on leveraging the process, are from Jim's consulting career. In the end we hope the reader will have gained some valuable leadership tools and ideas. In addition, there are examples on how the same process we learned forty years ago can help deal with an accelerated and ever-changing environment.

Chapter One

THE KENNEDY INCIDENT

USS JOHN F. KENNEDY

1990 DESERT SHIELD

August 10, 1990 began just like any other day on an aircraft carrier. It was a Friday and the talk was about the situation in Kuwait. On August 2nd the Iraqi army had invaded Kuwait. In response the United States, and the United Nations, began to impose economic embargoes on Iraq. There was speculation about what forces might be deployed to counter the threat. The aircraft carrier USS Saratoga and its battle group had already departed on August 7th for its regularly scheduled Mediterranean deployment.

Additional deployment was discussed but we did not really think that our ship, the USS John F. Kennedy (CV-67), would be on the list. We weren't the Navy's designated "ready carrier". No one on board seriously thought we would be called to go.

The only time we were scheduled to leave port was for the period from August through December 1990 for five one-week periods of carrier qualifications. As a matter of fact, as the Supply Officer (SUPO), I was most concerned with off-loading supplies from the ship in preparation for our four-month selected restricted availability (mini-overhaul) which was scheduled to start in January 1991. To minimize costs and the impending schedule, both the fleet and type commanders approved a "controlled stand down" of weapons systems, catapults, engineering equipment a reduction in endurance of provisions and even termination of stock replenishment of A-7 aircraft parts. Two of the ship's four boilers had already been "taken down" in preparation for the work to be done and a lot of other equipment had been dismantled. A significant portion of our crew was on summer leave.

The USS John F. Kennedy, now retired, was the Navy's largest conventionally powered aircraft carrier. It was a floating city of about 5,200 crew members and 80 – 90 aircraft of many different designations. It was longer than the Empire State Building is tall and about 23 stories high from keel to mast head. The flight deck encompassed about 4.5 acres. Everything an aircraft carrier does is on a much grander scale than most people imagine.

As Supply Officer, I was responsible for an inventory in excess of $250 million (125,000 line items), of repair parts for the ship and all aircraft aboard. In addition, I took on, and managed, all consumable supplies to support the ship's company, the Carrier Air Wing, and the Carrier Group Commander's staff. I was responsible for all of the "creature" comforts any city has; paying the crew, feeding the crew, the laundry, the ship's store, the barber shop, running the 262 officer stateroom hotel, etc. etc.

A lot can change with one phone call. At about 10:05 am on August 10th, I was talking to one of my friends about our weekend plans. I was complaining about the fact that the ship was not going to be doing much operationally in the next six months. This conversation was interrupted by a phone call from the Commanding Officer (CO). This call changed our lives forever. It went something like this:

CO: George, it's the Captain. How long does it take logistically to get the ship ready for deployment?

SUPO: Well Captain, you know we normally plan the POM (Pre-Overseas Movement) load out for a couple months and then accomplish the load out in about thirty days. Why, is there something I should know?

CO: I'm not sure right now. I'm on my way to an emergency meeting with the Fleet Commander. The rumor is that more ships are going to be deployed to the Gulf. I don't think it will be us, but you might want to start thinking about "what if".

SUPO: If we absolutely had to, I think that we could accomplish the load out in 2.5 to 3 weeks.

CO: OK, I'll let you know what comes out of the meeting.

Immediately, I called my division officers and leading chief petty officers into the Supply Office to brief them on the situation.

I'm a firm believer in upfront communication. We discussed my phone call with the Captain and a strategy to start building our plan. In a relatively short meeting, we discussed all the elements that went into planning the overseas movement load out. I directed the division officers to start reviewing those items that would be critical to a short fused (time limited) load out.

It was 1330 (1:30 pm) when the Captain called me again. His words were straight forward and to the point:

CO: George, it's the Captain. We have been moved up and will be one of the first deployers. Make all preparations for a full deployment load out.

SUPO: Do you know when we are scheduled to get underway?

CO: We will sail as early as the tides will permit five days from today on Wednesday, August 15th. We will have a department head meeting to discuss our preparations, but I thought you could use a heads up to get things rolling. Keep me informed and let me know if you need any help.

SUPO: Aye, aye, sir.

The Captain's direction to me, to make all preparations for deployment with an underway scheduled at first light on 15 August, launched us into a pre-overseas movement schedule that no carrier supply officer could have imagined. The next 96 hours were the most critical we had faced in our entire careers.

Our time for load out had been reduced from 30 days to 4.5 days. I called another meeting with my division officers and leading chiefs. Our department motto was "Nothing Is Too Hard" and we were about to put this to the ultimate test.

I told them that we were going to accomplish a full POM load out in the next 4.5 days. We needed to be fully stocked with enough provisions to feed, clothe, clean, and take care of the 5,200-man crew for at least six months. Even though we didn't know specifically where we were going, or for how long, we needed to think about items that would be critical to support the ship and air wing. We needed to review the ammunition allowance and perhaps order extra bullets and bombs. A full review of the spare parts requirements would be needed along with extra spare parts for the aircraft engines. The response from this group of junior officers and chief petty officers was incredible. The Food Service officer immediately handed me a stack of computer cards used for replenishment ordering that was over a foot tall. This represented his deployment load out requirement. Other officers were similarly prepared. I told them to brief the sailors in their divisions on our plans and to get started on their individual division work assignments... Oh yes, and there would be no liberty (time off the ship) until we had our load out plan established and underway.

Next, I called the Commanding Officer of the Naval Supply Center ("the world's largest store") to brief him on our situation and plan. He had previously been the Supply Officer of the Kennedy and we had served together at the Office of the Commander Naval Air Forces Atlantic. Our professional and personal association helped eliminate the normal red tape. I told him that we were scheduled to go Wednesday. He said he had already been informed and wanted to know what we wanted to load out and in what order. I told him that requisitions were physically on their way (this is before computerized ordering) and that we would like to load 1,000 pallets of dry provisions at 0500

(5:00 am) the next morning (Saturday). He said, "you got it, what's next". We requested frozen provisions, followed by consumables, repair parts, and then fresh provisions. He instructed me to touch base with the provisions people and the customer service people at the Supply Center to brief them on our schedule. Their response was equally incredible – "How much do you want and when?" they asked.

We started that afternoon with urgent calls to the outside vendors who made up our supply chain. We asked them to report aboard and help us determine items critical to our success. These included 'never out' items, repair parts for dishwashers, laundry equipment, and food items. In addition, we needed toiletries and uniform items for the ship's store. These were all items that we could not get from our Supply Center. To make matters more complicated we weren't the only ship getting underway on short notice. Our quick action, however, had allowed us to get our vendors aboard our ship while others were trying to contact them. From some of these vendors we took everything they had – candy, cassette tapes, cereal, salad dressing, underwear. They gave us a quick inspection of our galley and laundry equipment to make sure everything was in running order. The experience and solid recommendations made by our supply chain was invaluable in ordering and loading the right items. For example, we ordered extra ice machines, knowing their longevity would be compromised by a deployment to the Red Sea. We ordered three extra cash registers for the ship's store. Sure enough, three of the registers broke during the cruise.

To reframe our plan and strategies to meet the time limit imposed, I spent some time reviewing "deployment lessons learned" prepared by Supply Officers of other aircraft carriers. Learning from history and using the successful historical methods of others helped to shorten the time required to accomplish the load out.

At the department head meeting that afternoon, and with my new accelerated load out plan in hand, I briefed all departments on the schedule of events. The magnitude of this objective required a working party of several hundred sailors. We had to coordinate the delivery of provisions, parts, consumables, ammunition, and fuel while loading the 500+ personnel and their equipment from the nine squadrons of Carrier Air Wing Three, and the staffs from Carrier Air Wing Three and the Carrier Group.

The attitude of the John F. Kennedy's crew made this Herculean task achievable. At no time did anyone question whether we would be able to achieve our objective. It was a matter of putting our heads together, coming up with a plan to make it happen as efficiently as possible and ultimately find a 'better way'.

The following are edited excerpts from the book, *Hampton Roads in Desert Storm- A Star Spangled Salute*, by Betty Francis and Jack Dorsey.

> "The lists were endless, but the time wasn't. The supply department was on the piers that Saturday morning at 5:00 am meeting truck convoys that rolled into the Norfolk Naval Station. Other trucks and forklifts appeared from the Navy Supply Center not far from Pier Seven. There was near gridlock on the pier at times from all the supplies the vehicles were bringing.
>
> "I felt like an orchestra conductor," Sauer said.
>
> Sauer believes that it was the fastest full loading of an aircraft carrier in history. When his officers came to him at 6:00 that Saturday night to say the men were tired and needed a rest, Sauer couldn't allow them to stop.
>
> "It will be worse tomorrow," he recalled telling them. The crew worked until midnight, loading 1,000 pallets that

day. They were ordered to be back at 5:00 a.m. the next day. Another 1,200 pallets were waiting to be loaded.

In addition to the loading, we had the job of getting the supplies put away. It was an incredible effort. We knew if we didn't get the food put away on Saturday and Sunday, we were going to have a big problem. Once the ammunition started coming, the hangar bay would have gotten jammed up, Sauer said."

Four days elapsed and we had finished the load. This left us a short time in which to bid our families goodbye and load our own personal belongings for the deployment. Some of us even forgot to bring civilian clothes. At this point liberty in a foreign port was the last thing on our mind.

The fact that we were able to get underway on schedule the morning of Wednesday, November 15, 1990, fully deployed and endurance loaded, is a tribute to the dedicated sailors on the John F. Kennedy. It proved that in times of crisis, all elements can come together and get the job done.

There were a multitude of military organizations in the Norfolk area and Department of Defense logistics system and local vendors that were vital to us loading out in record time and getting underway on schedule. In that 4.5 day record making period the Supply Department, with the assistance of the entire crew, loaded over 2,100 pallets of its own stores and provisions, supported concurrent loading of the entire Air Wing maintenance pack-up and the Carrier Group Two staff pack-up for an additional 600 pallets. In the midst of this flurry of activity, a full deployment load of 500 pallets of weapons was loaded by Vertical Replenishment (VERTREP) and pier-side replenishment (INREP).

To make the task even more challenging, the Kennedy was berthed at the extremely narrow Pier Seven across from the USS Nassau. The Nassau was also preparing for deployment, and was loading MOGAS (combustible motor gasoline), which further restricted pier access. Many long-time stevedores at the Naval Base commented that such logistics activity had not been experienced since the Korean and Vietnam War periods.

This load out did not go without conflicts. We acknowledged this at the beginning of the process. For example, some felt it was against regulations to refuel, rearm, and load provisions and personnel all at the same time at Pier Seven. To overcome this objection, we met and came up with a safe solution that satisfied all regulations. We encouraged everyone to surface problems as they occurred. Every problem identified was met with a positive response and a solution soon appeared. Our success was achieved by working together using our personal and team resourcefulness.

This unscheduled deployment, to an unknown area, for an unknown duration, lasted 7.5 months from August 15, 1990 through March 28, 1991. During this period the John F. Kennedy had the highest readiness of any aircraft carrier deployed. During that 225 day deployment we did not lose any aircraft or lives. This is an incredible statistic in peacetime, let alone a war, where we flew 2,895 sorties, logged 11,263 flight hours and dropped 3,776,496 pounds of ordnance. This deployment was a testimonial to our competency in handling crisis situations.

We trained like we fought and fought like we trained. Our record setting time for a load out was a significant contribution to our overall success. If you had asked me before August 10, if I thought an aircraft carrier could accomplish a Pre-Overseas Movement load out in 4.5 days, I would have answered no. Cast into this crisis situation, however, this thought never surfaced. We had a crisis situation and we knew that working together, we could create a solution and lead our way out of it. And we did.

ANALYSIS

What type of limit did this crisis pose?

The limit forced on the situation by outside circumstances was one of TIME.

What was the traditional time limit associated with the Load out Process?

It was four weeks.

What was the limit posed by the situation?

It was 4.5 days.

This represented a productivity improvement challenge of removing 86% of the time from the process. A world class improvement was achieved, driven by crisis centered on a limit of time. The time saving solution was developed and led by one trained to deal with less-than-ideal circumstances.

In the next chapter we will present the Limit Driven Leadership Process (LDLP) that we have created from those first lessons we learned as plebes at Annapolis. This process will give you the tools that you need to deal with such challenges. Beyond this explanation of the process, the book will address several more challenging tales of crises driven by limits. After exploring these additional stories and analysis, the book will offer new territory that we feel will open opportunities for future gain beyond imagination.

CHAPTER TWO

THE LIMIT DRIVEN LEADERSHIP PROCESS

Developing solutions, in a limit driven crisis, requires an understanding of the basic elements of the approach. In crisis leadership, wisdom is primary, and intellect is secondary. It is a process where the "Big Picture Right Brain Thinking" trumps the logic and detail driven "Left Brain" point of view. This is the key to understanding the process. Here wisdom, a much used but not easily understood word, means the use of the power of the right brain functions to integrate your intellect, emotions and psychological self into a composite assessment and appropriate response.

Right and Left Brain – Two Ways of Seeing and Experiencing the World

What is right and left brain thinking all about? Basically, the right side of your brain controls the conceptual or comprehensive global way of knowing, while your left brain controls your logical and rational ways of knowing. While both sides control vital functions, your consciousness is primarily associated with the left side. This is because the left side is where your sense of clock time and your little voice of reason reside. Due to this fact the left side has played a dominant role in the skills necessary to successfully navigate in the industrialized world. Daniel Pink in his book, A Whole New Mind, *states that the future belongs to Right-Brainers. He believes that a major change is occurring whereby those that have succeeded in developing a dominant right-side capability will be able to see, design and create a far greater, more valuable culture and future for mankind. This is because the logical and rational way of knowing is not powerful enough, on its own, to solve the big problems of the day.*

What then are the attributes of this new and wiser way of thinking?

- It is seeing beyond the surface of a situation and allowing for a different point of view.
- It is allowing oneself to reflect before action, and to think deeper about a solution.
- It is to first be fully aware and understand what is happening before taking action.

- In the end it is a response built from insight and foresight resulting in the reframing of your initial point of view and actions in order to maximize the outcome.

If we were to lay out the process without this explanation it would appear to be quite linear. It is not. While a process proceeds step by step, the development of a solution to a crisis does not. Think about the times when you could not solve a problem and put it 'out of your mind' only to have the answer magically appear at some time in the future 'out of nowhere'. Actually, you only put it out of your conscious mind. It was sent from your conscious left-brain mind to your more powerful sub conscious right brain mind. There it was worked on 'offline' until the answer was fashioned and sent back over to your conscious mind for recognition and use. The answer did not magically appear. It was intentionally sent by you (the sub conscious you) to the conscious you as a gift.

This is the capability we all have but few recognize. The crisis leader, however, fashions this process into a powerful tool. The key process ingredient is the concentration on the need. In other words, the more focused your attention (AKA: concentration) the more energy you put into the process. The more energy applied the quicker the response. In the sub conscious the level of energy seems to determine the queuing order. If what is sent to the sub conscious lacks energy it may never result in an answer. Therefore, the key to using this process intentionally is to practice and develop your power of concentration. Our distracted world makes concentration more difficult. This is one of the reasons that we don't have more 'natural leaders' who can fashion constructive responses in our world of ongoing crisis. An effective leader understands this situation and manages their world in such a way as to avoid the 'noise' allowing for focus on the key needs and issues.

The steps that follow are provided as an explanation of the elements involved in what we call the Limit Driven Leadership Process (LDLP). It is not suggested that they be used as a standard step by step process. While the steps represent specific elements of the process, they do not always occur in a step-by-step manner. So, while these steps should be used as a training tool it is not suggested that a leader follow them in a strict manner. These steps must become engrained in a crisis leader and supplemented with concentrated energy. This is necessary so that the right brain can function openly and without the constraints imposed by a step-by-step approach to problem solving.

Wisdom, as the driving force behind this process, comes all at once. The solution is seen as a composite whole and not arrived at through long deliberation. Arnold Toynbee, in his famous *Study of History*, suggested a similar process used by great leaders he called "Withdrawal and Return". He suggested that great leaders, when posed with a problem, withdraw from the distractions of day-to-day life to concentrate on the development of a solution before returning with it for their people. Understanding this process can therefore enhance your ability to become a more effective leader.

THE LIMIT DRIVEN IMPROVEMENT PROCESS

LDLP consists of ten distinct steps. These steps are as follows.

The first five steps require concentration. The more concentrated energy you apply to these steps the better the potential outcome. Don't get distracted!

Step One – The Situation Analysis

What is going on and what has changed in terms of the limits associated with the task at hand?

Step Two - The Original Plan/ Process

What was, or is the original plan/ process, and what are the normal limits associated with it?

Step Three – New limits

What do you have to do and what is the gap between the original limit and the new one?

Step Four – Business as Usual – The Standard Approach (to close the gap).

What is the way that we normally do the task, achieve the objective or solve the problem? This is the standard frame of reference.

Step Five – Creative Compression - Reframe the Plan/Process

Think about the task at hand from a different perspective to develop new potential pathways to meet the challenge imposed by the new limits.

With step five the information and request are sent with concentrated energy to the sub conscious. The more energy (need) applied, the quicker the response. While your right brain does not work by the world clock (linear time), if you set a time requirement it seems to know when to get back to you! From step six onward you shift back to the rational left-brain mode of thinking.

Step Six – Selection Process

Select the best potential solution to the newly imposed limit.

Step Seven – New Plan

Embed the new solution to create a new plan for approaching the task.

Step Eight – Communication

Communicate the new plan to the stakeholders with the logic of the new frame of reference.

Step Nine – Deploy/ Execute

Implement the new plan.

Step Ten – Scorecard

Set up a scorecard or other device to measure the results.

_____
_____
_____
_____
_____
_____

Now that we have laid out the skeleton of the process how can you use it on a day-to-day basis to become a more effective crisis leader? As mentioned previously, depending on the nature of the crisis, many of the steps may be executed in parallel or may seem to occur simultaneously. For the purpose of explanation, however, the best way for us to convey an understanding of the process is in a linear left-brain fashion.

What follows is a deeper explanation of each of the ten steps. Included are some examples of each so that you can become familiar with the type of activity and work necessary to carry out this process.

Step One

The Situation Analysis

First, the leader must become adept at quickly analyzing the situation and identifying all the key elements. The mistake that most people make is to begin to get into all the details of the situation. This takes too long and is not an effective leader's point of view. While details are important, they are only secondary to the key elements associated with any situation.

One could call these the 'Big Picture Issues'. So, the first step is to take in and assess the situation from a big picture perspective. All great leaders are adept at taking in and quickly assessing the global nature of the situation. Look for the few rather than the many elements that make the difference between success and failure.

Step Two

The Original Plan/ Process

What was our original plan, or what process do we normally use, in these circumstances? How is this done in normal times? What are the key elements of the standard way that we do this type of plan or process? Again, the leader's point of view is focused on the key or critical elements as opposed to all the detail. A lot of leaders fail at this juncture because they begin to apply, or act, using their standard way of operating. They think that the way to succeed is to act immediately as this will give them more time to try to solve the crisis. Their answer is to work harder. This is a major mistake.

It is the same thought process that leads some to believe that working harder is more important than working smarter. This attitude is a heritage of our western philosophy and it holds us back. This is why some leaders perform better than others. As Toynbee suggested, they learn to reflect before they act. They look at what has happened and how it is normally addressed. The key is that they do not feel compelled to take action. They understand that their job is not to take action but to overcome a crisis. This is a big difference!

Step Three

The New Limits

What is the newly imposed limit? Again, the leader needs to assess this on a global basis. In the Kennedy story the new limit was obvious. It was one of time. The leader's problem was to solve or resolve the new time crisis. The Gap, as we mentioned in the first chapter, was 25.5 days (difference between traditional limit of 30 days and the new one of 4.5 days). Sometimes panic sets in at this juncture. If the gap is too large, or the time frame for fashioning a solution too short, panic can arise. When this happens, the leader may leap into action or withdraw and freeze. An effective crisis leader will do neither. An attribute of a successful crisis leader is one of accepting and welcoming great challenges. The greater the challenge the more they like it. They are never victims, but rather seek out and take on great challenges as a way of growing and testing their skills.

Defining the new limits, regardless of the magnitude of the change, provides the first jumping off point. The idea of a 'jumping off point' is critical. Again, if the leader jumps into action instead of jumping into creative thinking disaster can ensue. Also holding off the generation of new solutions until one has fully and globally assessed the current situation and limits is important. Error on the side of full preparation is critical at this point in the process to generate a successful outcome.

Step Four

Business as Usual - The Standard Approach

What is a standard frame of reference? For the purpose of this book it is the accepted way of doing something with associated standards of performance. The standard frame of reference in the Kennedy story was the accepted way of loading the ship in a 30-day period.

It was expected that if anyone leading the loading process followed the standard frame of reference map, or procedures, the ship could be adequately and safely loaded in that period.

All workers usually accept a standard procedure and are willing to follow the normal processes and work standards set forth for them. So, the crisis leader needs to fully understand the standard frame of reference to be able to see the basic framework.

Knowing what is normally done and being adept at it, is a skill that must be resident in any crisis leader. You must understand the underlying plan or process so well that you can, using wisdom, begin to work toward creative solution generation. To be most effective you must first be a student and know the innermost workings of the standard way of doing something.

As a leader you must believe that the standard way can always be improved upon. This is the last step in the preparation process. From here you move into the second and less defined jumping off point. You now move into the creative side of the process.

Step Five

Creative Compression - Reframe of the Plan/ Process

What do you do when you reframe the Plan or Process? It is not unlike reframing a painting. You can take a painting and reduce it, put a smaller mat on it, or otherwise change the point of view and impact of the painting and its various component parts. In doing this the artist is asking the question, "What would work better?" What would make a better statement? What would make a bigger impact? Reframing an existing plan or process is also an interrogative process. The crisis leader is asking questions about the elements, parameters, and existing understanding or viewpoint. Why are we doing it this way? Did we ever consider other ways? What is the real issue with the new limits that have been imposed? And most important of all, the leader brings to these questions a steadfast belief that there is always a better way! People will follow people who believe there is a better way and show a calm confidence in the face of crisis.

A good reframing will incorporate the new limits and will always do so in a way that adds more value as a result of the crisis. A new and better way will be found, and it will be found because of endless questions in pursuit of alternative solutions. A primary attribute of the crisis leader that aids in this part of the process is an innate or trained inquisitiveness. The need for this attribute cannot be understated. If you are to become a good crisis leader you need to have a strong inquisitive nature or desire to gain one. This inquisitiveness is where concentration and the development of the necessary energy behind the problem is generated. You need to see the world as full of endless possibilities instead of endless roadblocks. Excitement is the reaction instead of fear and frustration. The crisis leader anticipates the solution on the horizon and knows that its discovery is just a matter of exploring the possibilities. He or she knows that 'offline' their right brain function will fashion new and more effective solutions. They can literally feel it in their body!

Step Six

The Selection Process

How does a leader select the best solution? Most times the sub conscious will provide the 'best' solution, but other times multiple solutions will arise. They will, however, most often come as variations on a theme. There may be an instant recognition that one of the solutions best fits the needs of the crisis. The key as stated earlier is that the solution will add more value and is a better way. The necessary leader attribute for this stage in the process is that of insight and foresight.

The leader must be able to analyze the solution, or new way, not only in terms of its fit for the current situation but how it will impact the other areas surrounding it and the future. This requires both right and left-brain approach. Many times, a solution is selected and implemented with little time spent reflecting on its potential impact on other areas or it's 'downstream effects'. This can lead to an aborted solution for the current situation or long-term negative effects that worsen rather than relieve the crisis. So, the crisis leader must have a natural, or learned ability in this area. You must be able to mentally visualize the connections and downstream potential scenarios. This mental visualization is an important skill for anyone who wants to lead in this manner. Another consideration is what some have called the pursuit of the elegant solution. There are many definitions of an elegant solution but for our purposes it is one that uses only the current resources and limits any additional cost or resource need. Truly great crisis leaders can see how to use what they have in new or better ways to solve the problem. We will explore this idea in more depth later in the book.

Step Seven
The New Plan/ Process

Once the solution has been selected the leader needs to set forth the plan or process change in writing. There are two reasons for this step. One is to allow the leader to rethink the solution in more specific terms. The second is to create a document that can be used in the next step to communicate the plan. The personal leadership attribute needed here is one of plan and process development skills. In addition, it helps to have a heavy dose of story creation and telling skills. Storytelling and creation are the way effective leaders communicate and motivate others to change and reach new levels of performance. It is the way they inspire.

What is being done needs to be cast in heroic terms that give purpose and meaning to the new way. Dry or what we call 'cold' plans can leave the communication and implementation steps devoid of energy and direction. So, the changes need to be tied to higher purposes and prepared for clear and transparent communication.

Anticipation is another attribute that needs to be present. The leader needs to anticipate questions, concerns, and objections. Responses need to be crafted that add to trust rather than avoidance or sabotage. The skillful leader will take time to pause at this step and make sure that all has been thoroughly thought through. Again, you use foresight and insight skills to empathetically think through the impact and possible reactions from those being led. The goal of this step is to add confidence and a clear pathway forward.

Step Eight
The Communication

This is the step where the leader needs to listen as much as communicate. Too often the inexperienced leader will dictate the new way with little regard for its impact and resultant reactions. This is especially true when the leader is excited about having found a clear and fresh solution. Depending on the involvement of others along the way, and their prior experiences with the leader, there may or may not be enthusiastic support of the new way. Here the leader needs to understand two things. Change does not come easy and there are many ways to communicate. Change like all other human endeavors is a process. Like all processes those affected need some time to embrace the new way and fully understand how it will affect them. Unless the crisis requires an immediate response, such as in life and death situations, the leader will have to spend some time with those impacted to get them through the change. If this is not done, the leader will not have full cooperation and the new way will not find its way into the future work of the subordinates. It will just represent something done once, in order to get out of the crisis, but will lack any sustainable value impact. So, the need to communicate requires the leader to understand the power of the process of coaching subordinates through the process versus forcing them through it.

Secondly, there are different ways to communicate. This includes different ways that people learn and absorb new ideas. Some people are verbal, and others are more visual. Still others like to read and think through the changes. The tendency for any leader is to use only that method that best works for him or her. This is another mistake. A great leader will always use all methods of communication. In addition, the crisis leader will use redundant communication. We humans rarely 'get it' the first time. Effective leaders know this, cover all the bases, and repeat it often. They are also great story tellers. Through story they can effectively engage their followers with a memorable explanation.

Step Nine

The Deployment / Execution

As we mentioned at the beginning of this chapter, execution is where most leaders start. Since this is step nine in our process you can see that most leaders skip over, or miss all or a part of, the major foundational work for any successful crisis solution. No wonder there are so many failed plans and mishaps. While many crisis situations require a limited time response, the execution of all the steps still needs to occur. If the leader skips any one of them on the path to deployment, they risk the result of a bad outcome.

The leader, however, who has prepared and generated a new and effective solution, is ready to deploy and execute the plan. Here the leadership attribute is leading by involvement and if possible, by example. This is the first real test of truth for those being led. Does the leader believe in it enough to walk through it with us, or are we on our own?

The opportunity for the leader is to fully commit and perhaps even go to an extreme regarding involvement. This provides a visual impact and motivating force that can be gained in no other manner. There is no retreat or substitute for fully committed involvement in the process. The leader must be the first one on the scene and the last one to leave. The leader needs to carry the plan or process change with them and keep referring to it as he or she engages with their subordinates. This is where the leader animates the solution.

Step Ten

The Progress Report/ Scorecard

What are you going to measure to make sure that your new solution is meeting the requirement of the new limits imposed by the crisis? You don't have to measure a lot or make this complicated, but you must measure something to make sure that you are achieving the new level of performance required by the crisis. Here the leadership skill is one of the big pictures versus the small one. Details are not important.

What is important is the global objective(s) and success. In addition, you must measure the impact of the change on other areas in case you have not anticipated or thought them through correctly. You also must measure the impact on the future. This is important if the change is not one that is temporary but is to become the new 'traditional way' of doing. Feedback to the followers is a key and taking corrective action is a must. The awareness of where you are in the process and if your new way is succeeding are of utmost importance. If the new way is successful, this feedback can help to support the institutionalization of the change.

This concludes the explanation of the process, but it is only the beginning of the story. What follows are several more examples of limit driven crises from George's naval career. These, and their analyses using the LDLP, are offered to give the reader a broader and deeper understanding of the process and its applications.

CHAPTER THREE

THE NAVSTA KEFLAVIK INCIDENT

In 1982 our Naval Base at Keflavik, Iceland was strategically important. Upon my midyear arrival I became aware of many areas that needed improvement in the Supply Department. With an inventory of approximately $50 million, we had the responsibility to support the entire base and the deployed air wing. Our entire inventory was not properly stowed, and its validity was lower than acceptable. This resulted in degraded support to our customers through increased wait time, or non-availability of parts, and increased costs due to reorders. This situation had led to an increased level of frustration for all parties.

The Supply Department had identified a warehouse space shortfall of approximately 20,000 square feet. This shortfall suggested a need for a new warehouse that would cost approximately $4-6 million dollars. This would require a construction project that was "unfunded" for the current fiscal year and was not projected to be funded in the near future. The attitude that was prevalent was that there was not much that could be done until a new warehouse was built.

Utilizing a management style called 'management by walking around' that was popular at that time, I surmised that the perceived warehouse shortfall was not really as bad as had been documented. I knew that it was easy to make that statement but not so easy to make superiors or subordinates believe that I really understood the problem. Please remember this was the age before full use of computers. Unfortunately, there were no readily available computer programs to substantiate my beliefs. We had no programs that could calculate the storage requirement versus the storage capacity.

My visual inspection told me that the space was not being utilized very well. I also noted that items were not stored in a logical way. If they had been stored logically it would have made the management of 'fast movers' simpler, and inventory of all items very easy to accomplish. I had enough experience in inventory management, both shipboard and ashore, to know that my gut feel was correct. Shipboard life, and especially its space constraints, had made me more resourceful. I had to learn how to make the best utilization of space. I believed I could reutilize existing storage space by obtaining higher utility storage aids, changing the storage methods in the existing warehouses, warehousing affected material items, and then conducting a wall-to-wall inventory to establish a baseline. This sounds great but would I get my superiors and subordinates to 'buy-in'? There were lots of non-believers in Keflavik in 1982.

Initially I tried talking to them. Their reaction was for the most part negative. "You don't understand", "there just isn't enough space", and "that won't work" were frequent comments. In addition, not very many of my people believed my proposal could work. I decided the best thing to do was to give them a visual example. I would create a physical model to demonstrate how I had reframed and solved the problem.

My solution was low cost and simple. I surveyed the warehouse areas that I thought could be better utilized. While on the survey I documented the precise height, length, and width measurements of storage aids that were being utilized. Next, I took a very large piece of graph paper and laid out a scale model of the warehouse spaces that I wanted to modify. I had wooden sticks that were scaled to the stacking height that was available in the warehouses. I then used wooden blocks on the same scale as the graph paper to duplicate all of the various storage aids that were in use. I also replicated the amount of space required for material items that weren't physically warehoused (stored outside or in other non-desirable areas) or had not yet been received. Then I played around with the blocks in various configurations and found a couple different solutions. At this point in the process, I had reframed the problem which had led me to alternative solutions. The next step was to look at the viability and workload involved in relocating the racks and shelves. I then picked the best solution. This solution did require additional storage aids, but I had proved that the physical warehouse space was available if I could get the proper storage racks and shelves. Using my model, I briefed my superiors and subordinates on the plan. With this physical demonstration I was able to gain everyone's concurrence that my idea would work. Together we laid out a timetable to accomplish our goal. This included obtaining some new storage aids, relocating existing racks and shelves, warehousing items, stowing items that had previously been outside, and conducting a wall-to-wall inventory.

We identified the items that would be moved to new locations. They were removed and temporarily stored so that we could dismantle and move some storage aids. We were able to obtain the needed additional storage aids at no cost from the Defense Reutilization Material Office that was located on the base. After installing these new racks and shelves we restowed all items. In the process of restowing the items we utilized a new storage plan that considered fast movers and high dollar value items. This allowed us to better facilitate their management on a day-to-day basis. At the end of the process, we conducted a wall-to-wall inventory.

The need for additional warehouse space had been overcome with an elegant solution. Inventory accuracy increased resulting in decreased costs (less inventory losses, less reorder required, lower stocking levels required), improved customer wait time and faster response and improved employee morale.

INCIDENT ANALYSIS

Step One
The Situation Analysis

The leader used 'management by walking around' to quickly access the situation. He had already identified the needs as follows:

- Inventory properly stored
- Inventory validation (Is it right?)
- Increased support for the customer
- Decreased level of frustration of the stakeholders

With these four needs in mind, and as a result of his management by walking around, he had determined that the current space was not being utilized very efficiently.

Step Two
The Original Plan/ Process

The original plan was to build another warehouse and set it up to operate on the same basis as the existing warehouse. This solution would cost between four and six million dollars.

Step Three

The New Limits

The current warehouse had supposedly reached its limit and therefore the new limit posed was one of 'space'.

Step Four

Business as Usual - The Standard Approach

The standard approach was based on the standard method that was being used to store material and goods in the warehouse.

Step Five

Creative Compression –

Reframe of the Plan/ Process

Using the visual information gained on his visual inspection of the space, and his experience from shipboard life, he was able to reframe the solution from one of a new warehouse to a 'better use of the existing space'. Since this was a better use of existing resources, he had created an elegant solution.

Step Six

The Selection Process

He had modeled the existing space and developed several solutions. He then decided on the best solution based on what was the 'most viable' and on 'workload requirements'.

Step Seven

The New Plan/ Process

The newly designed solution, or plan, was to use new storage aids (available on the base at no cost), a relocation of existing racks and shelves, and re-warehousing the existing inventory including that which had previously been stored outside. This was all accomplished with a project plan. The last step in the plan was to create a full baseline on the current inventory.

Step Eight

The Communication

He was able to persuade his superiors of the viability of the plan based on the construction of a scale model. This model, and the accompanying project plan, was used to communicate the new vision to the superiors and subordinates.

Step Nine

The Deployment/ Execution

All of the plan was executed based on the project management calendar and he personally directed the execution of that plan.

Step Ten

The Scorecard

The newly documented inventory, and a system to maintain its integrity going forward, provided the scorecard for the solution and the sustainability of it into the future. He had made a contribution that created new value.

Key Questions for Additional Thought

1. What alternative frames of reference to solve a space limited problem can you generate?

2. What alternative solutions can you develop either from the story and incident analysis or your own frame of reference?

3. Based on your answers to the first two questions what solution or alternative solution would you select?

4. How would you have communicated to the stakeholders the changes suggested in the story?

5. How would you set up your scorecard for the new solution used in the story?

CHAPTER FOUR

THE ASHEVILLE INCIDENT

The USS Asheville (PG-84) was the lead ship of the Asheville class Patrol Gunboat. Originally built by Tacoma Boat Building of Tacoma, Washington and Peterson Boat Builders in Sturgeon Bay, Wisconsin, there were 17 Asheville class boats built. The original mission for these boats was as river patrol craft in Vietnam. When I was assigned to the Asheville in 1974 it was home ported in Guam, in the Marianas Islands. With a crew of only 4 officers, 4 chief petty officers, and 24 enlisted men, there were multiple job assignments for all hands. Officers and chiefs routinely performed duties normally accomplished by someone junior to them in a larger organization. On this smaller craft these additional duties were within their job descriptions. This did not create a training issue as they had all been previously trained on all these assigned tasks.

The Asheville class patrol gunboats were 164.5 feet long, with a 9'5" draft, twin variable pitch propellers, twin 725 horsepower diesel engines and an LM-1500 gas turbine (J-79 Jet Engine modified for marine use – same as F-4 Phantom jet). One of the Navy's fastest and most maneuverable ships, it had virtually all the functions of much larger warships and most of the capabilities.

Among the smallest of commissioned 'USS' ships in the United States Navy, we had all of the administrative requirements of a much larger ship. As with the rest of the crew the Officers and chiefs had many collateral duties. For example, I was the Executive Officer, Operations Officer, Electronic Material Officer, Combat Information Center (CIC) Officer, Communications Officer, Navigator, Personnel Officer, Administrative Officer, etc.

Our mission in Guam was maritime patrol of the Trust Territories of the Marianas. We performed humanitarian missions to many of the small islands and patrolled and protected the waters within the boundaries of the Trust Territories. In 1974, a decision was made to change the homeport of all of the PG's in Guam to homeports in the continental United States. The Asheville's homeport was to be changed to Chicago, Illinois.

The operations plan for the redeployment was developed. The 7 PG's home ported in Guam would transit across the Pacific Ocean from Guam to the Naval Station in San Diego, California where 2 PG's would remain in their new homeport. We would continue the transit down the coast of Mexico, through the Panama Canal, and proceed to the Naval Amphibious Base in Little Creek, Virginia where 2 of the PG's would remain in this new home port. The three ships left would transit up the Atlantic, down the St. Lawrence Seaway, through Lake Ontario, Lake Erie, and Lake Michigan, to our new home port of Chicago, Illinois. Our scheduled departure from Guam was 21 June 1974 and our scheduled arrival in Chicago was to be 28 October 1974.

Pre-deployment planning commenced with the additional burden of the requirements of a homeport change. This significantly increased the administrative workload. The entire crew became busy reviewing charts and operations plans, loading out required supplies and provisions, readying all equipment for the deployment, and performing all maintenance necessary to accomplish a cruise of 11,000 nautical miles.

On 21 June 1974, we got underway as scheduled. It was a very uneventful sortie from our homeport berth in Agana Harbor at Naval Station Guam. We proceeded out of port in a predetermined column and soon set about the routine business of the transit to our first stop of Pearl Harbor, Hawaii.

I was occupied reviewing operations orders, checking our navigational plot, and sending required Naval messages reporting change of status, when I was informed by the ship's hospital corpsmen that our lone quartermaster (the enlisted person in charge of navigation) was having a medical problem. Our corpsman quickly diagnosed the patient's problem and reported to me that he had suffered a mild heart attack. Although the quartermaster's condition was stable, the corpsman recommended that we take whatever action necessary to 'medevac' (medical evacuation) our quartermaster off the ship and return him to Guam. We were able to set up a helicopter transfer and he was successfully transported back to the Naval Hospital in Guam.

A crisis had occurred. We were beginning an 11,000-mile transit and we had just lost the only enlisted person qualified for navigation on our ship. The transit called for crossing the Pacific Ocean, transiting the Panama Canal, up the Atlantic Seaboard, down the St. Lawrence Seaway, and through the Great Lakes. Few sailors have ever had a chance for such an extended and challenging navigational opportunity. After conferring with the captain, I wrote a message describing this medical emergency and requested immediate replacement. This was standard operating procedure. Knowing this replacement would not be immediately available the Captain and I decided to implement an interim plan.

We were now resource limited and needed to reframe our problem. I was capable of doing the navigation, but I was also a bridge watch stander in 3 section duties (4 hours of watch out of every 12) in addition to my other 17 collateral duties. I simply could not be on the bridge all the time, so we needed someone else to perform the routine navigation duties. The solution presented itself in terms of alternative use of existing resources. I selected two of the enlisted men that I thought could be trained to perform navigation duties. These two men needed to be available to stand bridge watches, perform routine navigation duties, and be absolutely reliable. The two men I selected were a Fire Control Technician Gunnery (FTG1) first class petty officer and a Hospital Corpsman (HM1) first class petty officer.

The training was started and because of the enthusiasm and intelligence of the two individuals it proceeded very smoothly. As competence was demonstrated in each area of navigation, they were assigned routine navigational duties in the watch bill and stood their assigned watches. It was necessary to supplement the training as new circumstances arose. For example, arrival at Pearl Harbor and the transit of the channel required different navigational abilities than dead reckoning across the Pacific. In all instances, these two men adapted to the situation, were given the responsibility for the job, accepted the accountability, and completed their mission without incident.

We were underway for 70 days and had 13 port calls. All of this was accomplished without incident. Our two new "virtual quartermasters" continued to learn and increase their skill level. As they did this and performed flawlessly, they gained the confidence of the crew and the captain. In the end we arrived safely and on schedule in our new homeport of Chicago, Illinois.

Postscript:

In response to our first request for replacement we had been informed that there was no qualified person available for transfer to our ship. We were surprised to find the replacement, a Quartermaster Chief, waiting for us on the pier in Chicago. He had no idea of the opportunity he had missed for the "cruise of a lifetime".

INCIDENT ANALYSIS

Step One

The Situation Analysis

The only enlisted quartermaster responsible for navigation had suffered a heart attack. He was removed from the ship leaving no qualified enlisted person to navigate the 11,000 nautical mile journey.

Step Two

The Standard Plan

Alternate navigational duties between the two qualified crew members.

Step Three

The New Limits

The limit imposed in this situation was one of resources. The navigation resources available to the ship were now reduced below the minimum level.

Step Four

Business as Usual - The Standard Frame Approach

Without minimum resources the ship should return to port and wait for a replacement before proceeding.

Step Five

Creative Compression

Reframe the Plan / Process

Think in terms of raw resources instead of previously trained resources. Expand the thought process to include all resources and how they might be used.

Step Six

The Selection Process

Train one or more of the available resources in navigation. Due to the size of the ship most of the crew were already handling more than one job. This meant that they would not find it unusual to be asked to take over more or different duties. It was also a way for the selected crew to increase their personal value with a new skill in navigation.

Step Seven

The New Plan

Train two other individuals in navigation thus increasing the overall value of the crew and remain on course.

Step Eight

Communication

First the captain had to be convinced. Next a training plan was prepared. The crew to be trained was selected based on their previous record in terms of intelligence and attitude. Based on the solution presentation the Captain and I agreed on the experiment. The two men selected were then interviewed and their new potential job duties were explained.

Step Nine

The Execution

The training was split into two specific modules. The first and easiest was dead reckoning. The second involved more complex navigation in oceans, harbors and channels. A basic understanding of navigation terms, methods, and tools was covered at the beginning of the process. They were able to get their feet wet while dead reckoning their way to Pearl.

From there they were trained in the more complex skills necessary to navigate harbors and channels.

Step Ten

The Scorecard

Safely staying on course and following all rules of the road while navigating in ocean channels and harbors and arriving at their destination on time.

Key Questions for Additional Thought

1. What alternative frames of reference for a resource limit can you generate?

2. What alternative solutions can you generate either from the story and incident analysis or your own frame of reference?

3. Based on your answers to the first two questions what solution or alternative solutions would you select?

4. How would you communicate the changes suggested in the story?

5. How would you set up your scorecard for the new solution used in the story?

CHAPTER FIVE

LEVERAGING THE POWER OF LIMITS

We have taken a journey in the first four chapters that exposed the idea of crisis-imposed limits and a process for dealing with those limits. We have looked at three examples of the successful application of this process. All of this has been leading up to what we feel is the unrealized power of this process. We believe that this process can be leveraged by individuals and organizations interested in leading the way to the future. This is the opportunity before you.

The Opportunity:

To lead from within and apply the LDLP in a preemptive manner to situations where no current crisis but great challenge exists. The key is to apply the process at the challenge stage and not wait for it to become a problem or in the end perhaps a crisis.

Thus far in this book the motivation for change and adaptation has come from external or environmental stress in the form of a limit driven crisis. These forces for change have therefore come from the world and caused a reaction. What if you were to look inside of yourself and develop a list of the current challenges where LDLP might be able to cause great gains? Rather than using the LDLP to react you would use it to act. Often, we are sure, you have reviewed your actions in a crisis and seen where a wiser approach might have been a better way. Instead of reacting when a crisis occurs, what if you led with wisdom and stopped a problem or crisis before it occurred?

In the introduction to this updated edition, we mentioned that crises arise from a three-step process. The three steps are challenge, problem, and crisis. Every crisis starts as a challenge. If the challenge is not met, a problem arises. If the problem is not solved in a sustainable manner, then a crisis eventually occurs. What follows is an analysis of several real-life examples of situations from the perspective of this three-step process. What it shows is that if you were to address things at the challenge or problem stage most crises would never occur.

Navy Military Sealift Command (MSC)

The challenge for the Navy Sealift command is to be in a state of readiness/ preparedness to be able to act within 5 days to support the supply chain that feeds any projection of power that the armed forces might deploy. A recent article in the U.S. Naval Institute Proceedings sounded an alarm bell that this naval service was in a state of crisis. While the article did not specifically state the cause, it was obvious that over a period of years, and for various reasons, its needs, based on its mission, had not been met to maintain its standard state of readiness. If it were to be needed it would have to react due to a lack of resources. It would have to come up with a patch work set of processes to do its best to support any military action in the world. The Army also rang the alarm bell in Congress and said a Sealift shortfall would create unacceptable risk.

At the level of challenge Sealift must maintain its capability to meet its mission objectives. Somewhere along the line that level of maintenance deteriorated. People started doing the best they could with what they had and accepted the lack of support and direction (leadership). Not only was its capability deteriorating but it was not being enhanced or improved. The problem was not being addressed from the point of view of a sustainable solution. This has gone on for years until today, when the Commodore of Navy Sealift Command Atlantic and a Merchant Marine Officer wrote their article in the Proceedings. It is now a full-fledged crisis. The opportunity to avert a crisis has passed. It is time to react.

Epidemic on Board a Navy Ship

A pandemic can cause an epidemic aboard a Naval Vessel. That would be a risk assessment item that would need to be addressed in advance of a potential occurrence. Some Navy ships are as big as small towns, and the necessary close quarters make them a breeding ground for viral infections. At the challenge level this means that one must take actions to alleviate, or contain, the spread of a such a debilitating and destabilizing situation.

Civilian cruise ships insist during flu season that all passengers and crew observe strict hygiene protocols that limit the risk of on-board epidemics. Included are hand washing and sanitizing, shrink wrapped food stations and the use of gloves.

A recent cruise taken by Jim and his wife for 3 weeks, during flu season, experienced these strategies. Out of 2000 people on board there was not one trip to sick bay by either crew or passenger for flu or cold symptoms. The manager of the ship was proud of this fact. They let passengers know immediately, on embarkation, the importance of personal hygiene management, by handing each a spray bottle hand sanitizer for risk prevention. Is the Navy taking similar action when it is much more important for their crews to remain healthy in a much more confined environment? If these types of actions are not taken to thwart a viral incident, then it becomes a problem. The problem then becomes one of identification and containment. Protocols would need to be set up in advance to forestall any reactive on-board solutions. How to test, isolate and remediate any outbreak would be covered in these protocols. If within a given period of time the outbreak became too widespread, or was not contained, it would become a ship-board crisis and protocols would be in place to react to the crisis's situation. The famous John Paul Jones quote, now paraphrased, "People mean more than guns in the rating of a ship" should be kept in mind. They not only mean more but there is a moral responsibility to take care of the crew. Without work in advance, at the challenge and problem stages to ensure these ships have all the protocols and tools they need to protect their crew, the Navy is putting all crews in unnecessary jeopardy. It is further putting the ship captains in a position where their knowledge and capabilities would be taxed. They are sea captains and, even with their on-board medical staff, they cannot be expected to act as epidemiologists.

In a recent incident, where a naval captain felt compelled to send a letter (cry for help) through his chain of command to protect the health and well-being of his crew, it was evident that all of the aforementioned protocols were not in place. This problem became a crisis which was caused by a lack of preparedness and preparation.

Jim's 30th Reunion Story

After our 30th Reunion at Annapolis in 2000 my wife Ellie and I spent several days visiting the Sauer's in Virginia. One day George wanted to show us the 'Big Ships' and took us to the Norfolk Navy Base.

Upon arriving at the base, I felt that something was very different.

Then it struck me that there had not been a sentry where we entered the base. Further there did not seem to be any security in sight. I had grown up around military bases and this did not seem right.

As we drove through the base I remarked on this situation to George and he confirmed there had been a great change. It had happened after the fall of the Berlin wall. Feeling that for better or worse, we were no longer under dire threat by a superpower, the government had relaxed security. It had apparently been a budget saving strategy. The budget was saved at the expense of security for the people and other assets on the base. This was an example of lowering the standards to meet the security challenge. This immediately made security a problem.

While he and others had challenged this new point of view their challenges had gone unheeded. After traversing the base, we arrived at our destination. It was a parking lot on the far side of the base that was within several hundred yards of several nuclear aircraft carriers and submarines. We had arrived at this point unchallenged.

Except for a lone guard stationed on the gangway to one of the carriers there was still no security in sight. This confounded me. Why did I see this so vividly and react so anxiously?

First, I am sure that the mere absence of a "sentry at the gate" registered in both my conscious and sub conscious mind. Second, I am an artist and had just painted the Sentinel Tower Overlook at the Grand Canyon. As I painted it, I had thought about the symbolic nature of this structure and the presence of the American Flag on its peak.

As the right brain uses images to think these must have registered and become integrated thus sending me an immediate signal that a crisis might occur if this problem was not solved. It was the idea of the absence of a sentry. New limits had caused this crisis. Security had been limited although no crisis had yet occurred. A false sense of security had invaded our national consciousness but 9-11 was only a short time away. I had quickly arrived at step five of the LDLP. I had anticipated a crisis but was yet to act.

On arriving home, I searched the internet for evidence that I was not alone in my feelings. I found that I was not. Based on the amount of recent activity in the press, on just this subject, I relaxed. It seemed that others, far more powerful than I, had seen and were addressing this problem. It is here that I was wrong. My conclusion some years later is that we all need to take personal responsibility for adding to the 'voice of alarm' if we sense a potential crisis of any nature.

It is not someone else's responsibly. It is all our responsibility. We all have the power to foresee much more than we do, and it is critical that when we do, we do something about it. Regardless of the potential of the crisis we need to have the personal courage to lead from where we are and not assume that someone else will take care of it for us. (Note: Since the 9-11 attack security has increased significantly.)

What can we conclude from these stories? How often have each of us had these types of situations occur. We see an unattended challenge or problem. We see a potential crisis or a need for change and reform. Alarms go off, or a rush of creative adrenalin hits. What do we normally do? Normally, unless it is a life-threatening crisis, we do nothing. This also seems true for new opportunities. As in the Norfolk Story, we may initially remark on it to someone to see their reaction. We may in the case of a new opportunity 'run it up the flagpole' with a trusted friend or associate. In both cases the result usually leads to inaction. Why? We believe it is because of fear and laziness. We do not want to look stupid. Or more precisely our ego, in an ever-protective state, does not want to be challenged.

We convince ourselves that it is better to let the thought or idea 'go' and pretend that it never existed. We act as if we had never had the thought. We allow ourselves to be managed by other's opinions or the fear of ridicule. We want to be popular rather than effective. We shrink from our potential state of contribution to becoming less than we are to fit in and not rock the boat.

With this we lose our self-confidence and individual voice of authority. We lock up our wisdom, in the form of our powerful intuition and imagination, and at what expense? We are no longer capable of leading and so we complain. This seems to have become the human state of affairs, but it can be changed. The stories in the following two chapters are examples of how we might preemptively use our wisdom and add more value to the world.

CHAPTER SIX

THE APOLLO OPPORTUNITY

This is a postmortem on what might have been for the Apollo Space Program. What might have been had someone else, with a different frame of reference, been in charge? Freeman Dyson, in his 1992 book From *Eros to Gaia*, discussed what might have been achieved with the Apollo program had the planners reframed the plan. The program, which was considered a tremendous success, achieved the following results.

Apollo Program Accomplishments

Number of Missions and lunar landings:

6 Missions with 12 different Astronauts

Total Man Days on the moon:

36 Days

Man days on moon per ton of payload landed on the moon:

3 Days

Dyson went on to reframe the program based on the same resources.

The Reframe Premise: *Use half of the missions for astronauts and half for payload only.*

Using this new premise, the following would have been the predicted results.

Apollo Using Freeman Dyson's Plan

Number of Missions and lunar landings:

6 Missions with 6 Astronauts

Total Predicted Man Days on the Moon:

400 Days

Man Days on the moon per ton of payload landed on the moon:

40 Days

Dyson's reframe used the leverage of self-imposed limits on some of the variables. He took fewer individual Astronauts, but this resulted in more payload landed on the moon and more man days available. He felt that its success as a spectator event came at a great cost to science. We add that it also came at a high cost to taxpayers. With its lack of endurance, as a program, it greatly compromised the future of the space program.

This lack of program endurance came as there was no connection to the future. There was no pre-planned bridge to the next step in the adventure. When the interest for the Apollo Moon Show was over, and people stopped watching, the result was a loss of common purpose as regards Space Exploration. It was like a musician, with one big hit, that they constantly play until the public tires. With no songs to follow, the musician is soon forgotten. In this case the public saw little to gain from the repeat performances. It was a glorious dead-end street paved with good intentions.

In Dyson's book he relates how Werner von Braun had used a similar thought process years earlier when he envisaged the Manned Mars Project. Unlike the Apollo project von Braun did not start with the idea of simply getting men to Mars and back. Like Dyson he started with a frame of reference based on man days. To be able to achieve a reasonable study of the planet he wanted to have the mission stay 400 days with 50 people. He then determined that these first two parameters could be accomplished with about 150 tons of payload landed on the surface. So, his mission parameters were as follows.

Mars Using Werner von Braun's Plan

Number of Missions and landings:

1 Mission

Total predicated man days on Mars

400 Days

Man days on Mars per ton of payload landed on Mars:

130 Days

This is more than three times the increased man days on the moon suggested by Dyson. The power of starting with this frame of reference is that it puts the focus on being more resourceful. It therefore creates value. It has a built-in power that requires those involved to go outside of a traditional solution and use their creative powers to figure out how to achieve the visionary objectives.

So, these represent missed opportunities. It happens all the time. It happens because we often think only in one direction. This is the direction offered by traditional or known solutions. As we have stated in previous pages in this book, our minds are more powerful than that and have the capability of offering new solutions that are more productive and valuable. Here we offer two further thoughts on why we do not take advantage of this power more often.

- Our imagination has many powers and reframing with imposed limits is only one of them. This rarely occurs because we don't have to do it.

- If the challenge is not caused by an external crisis it is unlikely that we will proceed beyond an acceptable or traditional plan. This seems to be human nature

We seem to stop short of our potential when not externally confronted with a need to perform at a higher level.

An Aerospace Industry Story

Aerospace Manufacturing provides a good example of not acting unless you are forced to act. Once a computer program (CNC Program) is written and tested to manufacture an aerospace part it is rarely reviewed for improvement. What Jim has found, with his manufacturing clients, is that it is rare that a CNC program cannot be dramatically improved. It only requires that the programmer reframe the problem and create an improved solution. (To use LDLP) This rarely happens unless the customer demands price reductions (a crisis). What is lost? Productivity, profits, a more competitive environment, new jobs and the creation of new value is what is lost. If that is not enough to intrigue and motivate you then you need not read further.

So not having to do something, or accepting less than the best, is a condition of our human nature. How does one overcome this inertia? It must be accomplished via self-motivated leadership. As human beings, interested in progress, we need to lead. This leadership is only achievable through passion. Passion, or the self-motivating energy that it represents, is the doorway to self-motivated leadership and improved performance. How do you activate your passion? We believe that it is activated by emotion and not intellect. You need to get excited. Passion is not in the details but rather in the big picture. Remember the explanation from chapter two of the power of the sub conscious to create new opportunities and surprise us with the solutions?

It is this unexpected 'surprise' that will motivate. You can get excited when seemingly out of nowhere a complete solution emerges. Your conscious mind can then take over and work out the details. So, to lead you need to motivate yourself to begin to take on problems and issues using the LDLP. This is the pathway to the reframing process and its potential to unleash your passionate insights. Learn to reframe and you are on your way to becoming a more effective and passionate leader. The daily news is full of crises that can be used as 'homework' for gaining a powerful reframing competency. The bigger the crisis the better! Don't just read about the crisis and complain. Use the LDLP to reframe them and generate solutions. You will find that you will be able to generate many solutions regardless of the crisis or opportunity situation. Further, you do not need to be an expert in the area. The results will amaze you. Once you have gained competence in your reframing abilities begin to seek ways to communicate your new ideas. In other words, begin to do something with them. It is not important that you get a response or acceptance of your solution. What is important is that you gain confidence in the process and that you try. This is a pathway to personal leadership that will make you more positive and allow you to increase your potential contribution in all areas of your life.

Now let's return to our discussion on the Apollo Program. In the case of the reframed program, we could have gained a minimum value impact multiple of 13. What would we have found out? We may have been able to establish some form of permanent presence on the moon. This could have connected the original project with an enduring purpose and leveraged the original investment. How can you put a value on that possibility?

As stated in the previous chapter the unrealized value and power of this new process lies in its ability to create new value before a crisis occurs. This we call preemptive value, and it is at the core of our belief in the future value of this process.

CHAPTER SEVEN

THE INTERNATIONAL SPACE STATION OPPORTUNITY

In his 2003 book, *Leaving Earth*, Robert Zimmerman reported an interesting communication between Bill Shepherd, the first Shuttle Commander to approach the space station, and NASA. On his approach he reportedly commented to NASA that all they had to do was to send up some engines and give him the vector to Mars. What had Bill Shepard done? He had reframed the mission of the ISS as he first approached the station and radioed this message back to Mission Control. What he had uncovered was an opportunity, based on the idea of limits, which was not taken seriously by NASA. He had created potential for preemptive value.

The ISS, as with Apollo, appears to have become a dead-end program that is not connected to the future of Space Exploration or any greater purpose or meaning. While some science is being conducted it may be minor in comparison to the true value that the ISS could create as an interplanetary vehicle. As the station is already in orbit the large and expensive 'lifting' has been done. It is the victim, however, of a narrowly defined and isolated mission. Shepard, as a trained leader, had seen in a split second in his mind's eye the possibilities. He was trying to communicate and lead us toward a better use of current assets. While he was heard he was not taken seriously and to our knowledge he did not pursue this matter further. He had instantaneously worked his way through a portion of the LDLP presented in this book and had offered a new opportunity to the entire world.

Like Freeman Dyson, in the last chapter, Shepard had looked at the mission from a different perspective and had offered more value from his reframed insights. If something is going to come of his insight it cannot stop there. Someone needs to lead and do something to communicate and explore this potential opportunity.

As suggested in the last chapter someone would have to get passionate about this opportunity to lead beyond the mere creation of the idea. At this point we are through step five in the process with the reframed ISS opportunity. In step six options would be selected to bring the reframed idea to reality. The following are two potential step six solutions suggested by this new insight.

Solution One – Based on the insight rewrite the published NASA Strategic Plan to show the potential gains from the new idea and send this plan to all stakeholders.

Solution Two – Develop a project task list to convert the ISS to an interplanetary vehicle and send this project plan to all stakeholders.

Why would one do this? As in the examples in this book, the leader who generates the new idea needs to be able to convince all stakeholders that the new idea is worth pursuing. This is where the leader must become persuasive, and it is where the solution application details come into play. (Remember the model developed to portray the solution to the storage problem in Keflavik.) As this requires a lot of work many will beat a hasty retreat to the status quo. The preemptive crisis leader will not! The self-motivated energy emerging from the passion for the idea must be enough to carry the leader through this part of the process. At this point it is doing something for the sake of doing it and not because one has to do it. Doing it because it is the right thing to do becomes the internal force driving the preemptive crisis leader. It is a part of their Leadership Lifestyle.

Moving beyond Shepard's insight to action the following summaries are offered as a set of plans (step seven of the LDLP) to modify the NASA Strategic Plan and/or implement a conversion of the ISS.

NASA Revised Business Plan Summary
Originally developed, with input from other sources, by Jim Hull in February 2004

Summary

This strategic Plan is written as a response to NASA and the American People to move forward with a more focused and beneficial space program. Realizing that there are many ways to move forward this plan is offered as a structure that responds to the challenge in such a way as to overcome traditional opposition and add value. It does this in the following manner.

- The recognition that NASA is not an administration company but rather an exploration company.
- Recognition that there must be a Master Project that ties all other projects to it as subsets. This provides focus and relevance to both NASA and its purpose.
- The budget should be approached in terms of investment and value rendered.
- The industrial support structure (Supply Chain) needs to be integrated for greater value.

- The recognition that there are alternative methods of accomplishing missions with an emphasis on greatest quality for the least investment.

The Vision

NASA is the primary public space exploration company dedicated to the manned and unmanned exploration of all physical territories beyond earth for the benefit of mankind.

The Purpose

The purpose of exploring territories beyond the earth is to learn more about ourselves, our origins, the workings of time and space, resources known and unknown and to pave a road for futures possibilities based on these discoveries by inspiring the human soul through accomplishments of goals of a very high order.

The Master Strategy

To achieve the vision and purpose, NASA will focus its resources on the development of a manned exploration system of the solar system.

ISS Mission Plan Profile

Purpose: To develop a plan to create a mission to use the ISS as the initial primary instrument for moving beyond earth orbit with L1 (gravitationally neutral point between the earth and moon) as the initial objective, the moon as an intermediate objective and Mars as the ultimate objective in such a way as to leverage the sunk cost of the ISS and create more value for all stakeholders.

The Major Plan Elements

1. ISS – the vehicle
2. The Human Factor – The manned mission considerations.
3. The Mission Profile/ Plan – The milestones and objectives.
4. The Space Corridor – The economic infrastructure.

The Plan Elements by Category

1. The ISS
    a. Structural Survey
    b. Proposed Structural conversion process (all or part)

    c. Propulsion system requirements/ proposed design.

    d. Guidance and telemetry requirements.

    e. Shuttle or secondary intermediate transportation system (To and from the ISS and the terrestrial objects) requirements.

    f. Flow chart process and create PERT Chart for all key work elements.

    g. Cost/ budget factors associated with the conversion and mission.

    h. Risk Analysis and mediation factors.

2. The Human Factor

    a. Environmental requirements based on Mission Plan.

    b. Specific Bio/ Med considerations

    c. Cost/ budget factors associated with the conversion of the ISS.

    d. Flow chart process and create a PERT Chart for all key work elements.

    e. Risk analysis and mediation factors.

3. The Mission Profile/ Plan

    a. The three-step objective process/ L1, Moon, Mars.

    b. Sub objectives at each stage where L1 and Moon objectives ties to a successful Manned Mars Mission.

    c. Sub objectives for terrestrial exploration.

    d. Time elements set against a multi-year plan objective.

    e. Key all mission profile objectives to work on ISS and Human Factors.

    f. Overall Risk Analysis and mediation factors.

4. The Space Corridor

    a. The business model – A cooperative interdependent economic model made up of business, government, and academia.

5. The Plan to Plan – People and Organization

    a. Objective: To recruit a project development team that can complete a proposal to covert the ISS from a stationary space station to an interplanetary vehicle in such a way as to leverage the sunk cost thus creating new value and a more compelling mission for the ISS assets currently in orbit.

b. Initial list of Jobs by Category

   i. Structural Engineers

   ii. Space materials science and engineering

   iii. Propulsion Systems

   iv. Navigation, Guidance and Telemetry

   v. Vehicle Systems Engineers

   vi. Mechanical and Electrical Engineering – Space Vehicles

   vii. Space Biology

   viii. Astronaut Environmental Support Systems

   ix. Astronaut Safety and Escape systems

   x. Shuttle Vehicles/ Pod Design and Construction

   xi. Quality

   xii. Safety and Risk Management – Space Systems

   xiii. ISS Design, development, and construction knowledge

Organizational Design Strategy: Create a traditional functional organization with a matrix project management team.

Some progress has been made since the creation of the return to space plans set forth in 2004. What was done with these plans? Nothing. What has happened some sixteen years later? Former President Obama and President Trump suggested a similar plan. They have not, however, suggested the bold move to use existing resources in the form of the ISS. That is now our responsibility, and we continue to pursue it with passion.

Why is this so hard a lesson to learn? What is standing in our way as these types of opportunities arise? This is what we will discuss in the next chapter.

CHAPTER EIGHT

THE TRANSFORMATIONAL MODEL

In the last three chapters we hinted at the real power of limits driven leadership. This chapter will pick up where we left off ten years ago and provide a more comprehensive Transformational Model. It is a top down, strategic and global model for improving anything and everything in the world.

This is a new way of thinking for most people and requires an active imagination. Some of the earlier chapters referred to the left and right brain way of processing information provided from the external world. We suggested the use of imagination to create solutions for crisis driven situations. Building on this idea we will now explore how to approach and improve your job, your life and that of others by avoiding crises.

The Transformational Model Processes

1. What - What are you trying to improve?
2. Current State - What are the current levels of performance for the area that you have chosen to work on?

3. Future State - What are the levels of performance that you want to seek?
4. GAP - What is the GAP between the answers to questions 2 and 3?
5. Change - What changes will you make and what will you have to invent/create to reach the new levels?
6. How - What is your implementation plan for the developmental work required to reach the new levels of performance?
7. Communication - How will you communicate your changes to motivate and influence those involved?
8. Measurements - How will you measure progress toward your goal?

This process is similar to the bottom-up Limits Driven Leadership Process (LDLP). The difference with the Transformational Model is that YOU are deciding to improve performance. You are not being driven to react to a crisis. You know that waiting to react to a crisis is not acceptable and is too slow for progress in the real world.

What follows is an example of how this transformational approach could have been used in the incidents covered in the opening chapters of this book.

The Kennedy Incident

What would have happened if instead of an externally created crisis, George had arrived at the Kennedy and on his own during dry dock, shortened the load out process? Process improvement was the way he approached any new assignment, and it might have looked something like this...

1. What to improve? - Improve the time for the Load Out Process
2. Current Level of performance – 30 days
3. Desired Level of Performance – 5 days
4. Gap – 25 days
5. Changes – Review and remove process waste from each of the processes associated with the load out. Where possible integrate processes and flow. Review the shipboard storage plans. Integrate process changes with manpower requirements. Work in conjunction with suppliers to improve coordination and support. Create a 'Just in Time' ordering and delivery process. Invent new tools, systems and processes to permanently enhance the load out operation?
6. Implementation Plan - Create a load out Improvement Plan and Executive Summary (PERT or Gantt chart?) to present to the Captain and other interested parties. Prepare a staff and supplier implementation plan.

7. Communication - Send a proposal to the Captain and all interested parties.
8. Measurements - Progress to be measured by weekly Key Performance Indicators and progress Reports.

(Note: None of the above type of work is usually a part of anyone's job description. It is the type of work that is taken on by one who has chosen a leadership lifestyle. This person knows that increasing levels of performance is more important than simply administering current operations daily. It is a way of transforming the entire operation.)

In the case of the original crises another application of the above model could be a postmortem review (improvement capture) of the actual new ideas. What was learned in the process of successfully conducting a load out in a shorter period? What lessons were learned; what patterns were uncovered for improved productivity? How could this be applied to the current way of loading out for all aircraft carriers? (For all ships?) You can see that this type of improvement has a potential global impact that makes everything run better forever! A leader thinks in terms of not just the impact of their job (Head Supply Officer on the Kennedy) but rather their impact on the whole enterprise (The Fleet). Their current assignment is just the 'test kitchen' for the entire organization. How good can we get? How much increase in performance is possible? What improvements can we share with our fellow sailors?

The Self-Fulfilling Prophecy Effect – We have both found in our careers that if we could imagine something, we could make it happen. Whatever improvement in performance we have been able to imagine we have been able to achieve. There are physical limits to be considered but the ability to improve is almost unlimited. If you can dream it, you can make it happen!

The NAVSTA Keflavik Incident

As with the Kennedy Incident what would have happened if George had arrived at his new post and decided that he needed to expand the internal storage capacity of the current facilities. He knew that they were never optimized, and he wanted to make them more valuable. He had not been asked to do this, and it was not a request of any external authority in his command structure. He simply knew that no matter what assignment he was given, he was going to improve all of the resources under his command.

> Step One – What to Improve – Storage capacity of current facilities.
>
> Step Two – Current Level of Performance – 100% capacity with existing storage strategy.

Step Three – Desired Level of Performance – Expand current storage capacity by 50% using existing structures.

Step Four – GAP – 50%

Step Five – Changes – Find or invent new storage methods and strategies.

Step Six – Implementation Plan - Inquire from other facilities, research civilian methods and strategies, review the current list of stored items for those no longer used or needed. Conduct brainstorming sessions with current personnel. Set time limes for implementation.

Step Seven – Communication - Present Executive Summary of proposed plan and timeline to command. Review with staff – written and meetings.

Step Eight –Measurements – Measure progress against the implementation plan with weekly updates. Measure the improvement of storage capacity at end of project.

As with the Kennedy Crisis situation and improvements a postmortem of the methods and strategies used to overcome the crisis situation would have revealed a number of new 'best practice' ideas and methods for shore based operations and the Fleet in general.

The Asheville Incident

What if George, when he arrived at his new command of the Asheville, did a quick risk analysis? It was one of the first things he always did at a new assignment. From this analysis he decided that one of the main risks was the lack of depth of personnel. As a small vessel the crew was minimal for all positions. In this type of situation (also holds for small civilian businesses) one of the greatest risks is loss of human resources for any reason. This is especially true for essential staff that can bring the operation to a halt. Recognizing this risk, he put together a plan to neutralize it.

> Step One – What to Improve – Increase depth of manpower resources using current resources.
>
> Step Two – Current Level of Performance – 100% staffed with no depth per position.
>
> Step Three – Desired Level of Performance – 100% back up for all mission critical duties.
>
> Step Four – GAP – 100% increase in capacity for mission critical duties.
>
> Step Five – Changes – Expand capacity of current personnel.
>
> Step Six – Implementation Plan – Cross Train current personnel to back up on essential/mission critical duties.

Step Seven – Communication – Cross training Plan with sign offs and timelines. Proposed Plan to command for approvals. Communicate in writing and verbally with existing crew.

Step Eight – Measurement – Meet timelines with sign offs, weekly review meetings and updates.

If this plan were implemented and worked, it would lead to the possibility for a major increase in risk aversion for the entire fleet. These are projects taken up by leaders, both military and civilian that lead to sustainably new and better ways of doing everything. Leaders following their chosen Leadership Lifestyle see this as a 'given' in terms of every job they ever do.

(Note: Your most valuable employee may be the one that can do 'everything'. Do you have one of those? It is unlikely in this era of specialization.)

How does this approach apply to civilian organizations?

The following is an example from Jim's work as a business consultant. It is a general area of performance that exists for all 'for profit' companies regardless of their size. This area is that of productivity. One measurement of productivity is sales per employee (SPE). This is calculated by dividing the gross sales by the number of employees in the organization. The question that it asks is how productive are we on an individual employee basis? What follows is the eight-step approach that a 'for profit' company might follow to figure out how to permanently increase the average sales per employee.

> Step One: What to improve: Sales Per Employee
>
> Step Two: Current Level of Performance - $125,000
>
> Step Three – Desired Level of Performance - $250,000
>
> Step Four – GAP - $125,000
>
> Step Five – Changes – Implement Performance Based Employee Compensation Plan (PBC). Implement Process Improvement Plan. Train all employees on Process and Individual Productivity Improvement. Create a 'list of the obvious' changes that can be implemented in the short term to get the improvement plan underway. (Note: This is a list of things that have been known for some time but have not been implemented to date.)

Step Five – Changes - Create a Pro Forma PBC Model and Process Maturity Plan. Conduct Training Sessions for all staff.

Step Six – Implementation Plan - Provide sample PBC Plan and Process Improvement Models to all employees.

Step Seven – Communication - Post improvement results weekly.

Step Eight – Measurements - Set weekly goals for SPE, freeze employment of new employees and allow the current employees to improve productivity to grow into the new sales results. Allow them to share in the gain as they go. (Quarterly calculation and payout of % of improvement in KPI).

Jim used this process as a win/ win (Owners and Employees) solution for several clients. The owner(s) would first set the proposed targets in terms of SPE. They would then work with the employees in a 'partnership mode' to improve results. Along the way the employees and management would share in the gains in productivity (measured by SPE). As a result, the organization would permanently change their culture and levels of financial performance. They would also increase the Business Value of the organization. Using this process one of Jim's clients set new benchmarks for SPE for their industry.

(Note: As most industries post the average SPE these could be used to both measure current performance and set new targets to outperform the industry.)

Applying this process to a 'for profit' business may require a reorganization of resources to improve flow and get rid of waste in key processes. In his consulting business. Jim did this for several insurance organizations using a manufacturing model. Most manufacturers are familiar with the 'cell model'. This is a model that creates a better flow of inputs to outputs by arranging the resources differently. Basically, a cell is built with all the necessary equipment in a particular arrangement. (Example: U shaped arrangement of equipment on the floor). Once completed a team is assigned to the cell and trained to work the stations in the cell. They are all cross trained! The raw material flows into the input side of the cell and flows from station to station until it becomes the output. This creates a flow of parts coming out of the cell. Most cells are designed to accommodate a certain 'family of self-similar parts. This arrangement is the most efficient for certain types of manufacturing operations. Using this concept for insurance organizations Jim set up both Underwriting Cells and Customer Service Cells. By so doing he was able to more than double the capacity of both types of operations. The conversion process looked something like this:

Step One – What to Improve – Output of a group of fixed and human assets.

Step Two – Current Level of Performance – Given at 100% with the current organizational design.

Step Three – Desired Level of Performance – 200%.

Step Four– GAP – 100%

Step Five – Changes – Reorganize current resources in a cell designed to improve flow of end product(output)

Step Six – Implementation Plan – Design cell with current resources. List step by step changes to reorganize. Cross train all team members to be assigned to the cell. Identify team member expertise by task. Assign each employee to a workstation in the cell that most closely fits their area of expertise.

Step Seven – Communication – Set up an Executive Summary with examples of how the new cell will work. Present to owner(s) and direct reports. Achieve buy -in for all changes.

Step Eight – Measurements – Set goals for transformed cell performance. Establish weekly Key Performance Indicator (KPI) on outputs to measure progress and report to staff and management.

What this represents is an example of how an idea from one industry can inform another. All businesses have processes they follow to move their inputs through a value stream to create outputs. Therefore, most organizational design solutions are applicable regardless of the industry. They merely must be modified by industry, but their underlying essential elements usually remain the same.

Discussion

These examples exemplify the idea that all our activities are processes, and all processes can be improved. Processes developed by human beings are never optimized. They are usually developed until they meet the minimum criteria for application and implementation. This usually creates waste as they are not optimized. The leader knows this and uses this lack of 'finish' to improve all that they touch. This also applies to products and services. For example, an internal combustion engine is a product and a process. It has inputs and outputs. Unfortunately, one of the outputs is pollution so in process jargon it is a non-optimized process. It creates waste. Faced with this situation what have engineers done about finishing the internal combustion engine process? They have changed it and made it more complete. By designing a new internal combustion engine that uses pressure to burn almost all the fuel, the new model produces more fuel efficiency and virtually no pollution. Most people do not know that this new engine is currently in limited production. As a disruptive new technology, it will take time for refinement and acceptance, but it exists and improvement in the internal combustion process is well within reach.

Elegant Solutions – Elegant Solutions were mentioned earlier in this book in the chapter on the LDLP. We bring them up again in this chapter because of their importance. A good example of an elegant solution is the use of cell design discussed earlier in this chapter. As this example revealed, elegant solutions cost little if anything to implement. Elegant solutions are the ones that you should generate when working on performance improvement. It is easy to spend money to improve things with more, better, or different resources. Elegant solutions are a form of alchemical or 'something from nothing' type of approach that enhances your contribution. It has been our experience that elegant solutions exist for most situations. Go for these first before you make investments in more, new, or enhanced resources.

What processes are you responsible for? What areas of performance do you want to transform? What new improvement levels would you like to achieve? The only thing stopping you is time and your own desire, discipline, and effort. Are you a leader? Have you decided, or are you already living the lifestyle of a leader? That is what we will discuss in the next chapter.

CHAPTER NINE

THE LEADERSHIP LIFESTYLE

As we mentioned in the introduction to this new edition, one is not born or trained into leadership. Leadership in our opinion is a lifestyle that a person chooses. But how does a person who wants to consider embracing a leadership lifestyle proceed? The following is a 10-step process for constructing a personal Leadership Lifestyle Map.

Step One –FOCUS - Are you ready to dedicate yourself to improving everything that you are responsible for in your life? (Even if nobody asks?)

Step Two – TIME – Are you prepared to focus a larger portion of your time on improvement projects?

Step Three – PASSION - What areas are you most interested in improving performance? Are you prepared to develop an improvement plan and implement it in these areas? Are you prepared to act?

Step Four – CAPABILITIES - What are your key skill, knowledge and experience areas?

Step Five – GAP - Do the answers to step four align with your areas of performance enhancement in

Step Three? If not, are you prepared to bring them into alignment?

Step Six – DISCIPLINE -Do you have good work habits? If not, are you prepared to improve them?

Step Seven – PERSONALITY - Are you a balanced personality in terms of the point of view of being both a 'people person' and a 'transactional person' in your relationships? Can you shift your focus between these two points of view depending on the situation? If you are out of balance between these two are you prepared to change and bring them in balance?

Step Eight – LIFE -Do you have a balanced life in terms of work, play, and family? Do you have consistent values for all three? If not, are you prepared to change to a more balanced life?

Step Nine – CHANGE - Are you a change catalyst? If not, are you prepared to become one?

Step Ten – CHARACTER - Is character important to you in terms of being trustworthy and compassionate? Are you generous and appreciative? If not, are you willing to become more so?

DISCUSSION

The importance of each of these items for a leadership lifestyle is self-evident. The key is that each of the ten steps are equally important. if you answer 'no' to any questions asked you compromise your ability to lead. A single 'no' means that you cannot live a leadership lifestyle. In our opinion, even if you have been given a position considered to be a leadership role (positional leadership), you will not be capable of performing competently if you have not answered yes to all these questions.

In addition to the construction of a leadership lifestyle, all leaders help others to lead. This is accomplished intentionally with exposure to the leadership lifestyle and approach. It is also accomplished through leading by example. This is the trust builder. You will create future leaders out of followers if they can trust that you do what you say you will do. It is not enough to have followers. A leader is aware of this fact. It is in the conversion of followers to leaders that the process adds value. In this way the leadership lifestyle provides fertile ground for the development of future leadership talent.

A Leadership lifestyle may seem easy to follow. This is because it requires only one point of view. This point of view is defined by high values exemplified by actions and continual improvement of everything. This is simple to understand but difficult to accept, embrace and follow. As we stated in the introduction it requires courage.

The idea of courage wove its way through all our instruction and indoctrination on the subject of Leadership at the Academy. At a young age that translated to a willingness to go in harm's way. Now, on reflection, we understand that courage goes beyond just the obvious. It requires courage to always go as far as need be to change something for the better. This is a war waged against the status quo. It is a war against the status quo thinking that is comfortable but always creates crises. Those who put themselves on the line for performance improvement, and never rest until improvements are made, are true heroes. They are the ones that we can thank for a future that is brighter and better. They too are warriors as they fight for a better way of doing everything.

This 'everything in the world' can be seen in terms of processes. Every process created by man is headed toward crisis. Those who have chosen a leadership lifestyle are capable of reacting to a crisis or heading one off. The top down and bottom-up processes for achieving these improvements are ways of improving value stream processes. A leader sees their worth and work as creating better and more effective value streams. They improve the value of every process they decide to work on or react to. In so doing they are constantly working to move from the current state of a value stream to the future state.

They first identify the future state and then work back to the current state with new value add process steps. Along the way they engineer out waste and improve resource use. They finish incomplete processes. This is the major work element of a leadership lifestyle.

The Leadership Lifestyle includes an awareness, by the leader, of the need to operate from the middle point of view. We live in a world of opposites. The famous Yin/Yang image depicts this reality. To operate effectively, influence others and achieve progress toward a better future state, the leader understands the wisdom of this diagram. The leader realizes the need to operate from the middle. While their personal point of view may be located to one side or the other of the symbol, they understand that to make progress they need to make a connection with those who are on both sides. Thus, there is the little dot of white in black, and black in white, in the Yin/ Yang diagram. They need to be able to adjust, learn and have empathy for other positions and ideas. They can only do this from a point of view between theirs and the other. A leadership Lifestyle requires this agility, effectiveness, and competence. It is inclusive and not exclusive. It is dependent on it. It is also the most powerful point of view. it includes not only those that see the world from the leader's perspective but everyone else who does not. This power allows the leader to be a bridge and not a wall. It fosters progress and flow of ideas and improvements rather than a stalemate created by those who defend only their point of view. If the leader's new ideas and value stream improvements are to make their way into the light of day, it requires the middle point of view to get there. In every situation they must respect the other side to foster change and make progress.

In the end it is a choice. Only you can decide that you want to add value to the world and overcome the negative impact of crises. Only you can decide to be a force for positive improvement. In so doing you become a force that works on the world by working with the others that live in it. It is a belief in yourself as a leader that will make the difference and create your destiny.

> Your beliefs become your thoughts
> Your thoughts become your words
> Your words become your habits
> Your habits become your values
> Your values become your destiny
> --*M. Ghandi*

CHAPTER TEN

CONCLUSION

We are sure as you read your way through this small book you recognized some familiar territory. Perhaps it reminded you of situations where you were more or less resourceful. This is becoming a more familiar idea in an age of abundance. Doing more with less, or succeeding without, is not how most of the living human beings in the developed world have thought until today. The new green movement, as one example, is reversing this thought process. Focused on reducing, reusing, and reapplying resources is its goal. In addition, some of our greatest and most heroic moments, have come when the job was accomplished with fewer resources. As an example, the resourcefulness of the Apollo XIII crew comes to mind.

We have all been conditioned to accept less than optimum performance. Jim, in his consulting business, has encountered many non-client business owners who were not motivated to do their best because they could do very well with a mediocre performance. The external limits placed on them were not challenging enough to motivate them to improve. So, they could get by, and sometimes do well, without continuous improvement. Instead, they worked hard to maintain the status quo. In the end they were not willing to put in the extra effort to be the best and adapt a leadership lifestyle. They lacked the courage.

We believe the issue of why we do not choose the leader's lifestyle is the way we THINK. We think that we are in control of our thought processes, but we are not. Cultural conditioning and indoctrination into ways of thinking (channels) impede abilities for most of us to see new and better ways to do things. In some cases, this freezes people who face crises because they not only don't know what to do but have little belief in their ability to act effectively and lead the way out.

Learning to think differently is the goal if you want to live a leadership lifestyle. The wisdom based right brain process (LDLP) and the Transformational Processes are just two ways to think differently. We hope that they will begin to open your mind to new possibilities. Here are some goals and hopes we have for your future.

- Realize your potential for contributing much more than you do.
- Begin to use your right brain (the forest) to lead and not be led by your left brain (the trees).

- Never let an insight or foresight go unattended.
- Improve everything you can and help avoid crisis situations.
- Lead and introduce others to a leadership lifestyle.
- Learn to trust yourself more than the opinions of others and lead with the confidence of your convictions.
- Be courageous and a warrior of the new! Fight for a better way of doing everything. Your life and that of everyone else depends on it.

Our introduction to limits and crisis leadership began at Annapolis fifty years ago. We hope this book launches your ship in a similar direction and that you have clear skies and full sails leading you to discover new lands of opportunity!

FURTHER READING

These were mentioned in our book and are worth further exploration and reflection.

Hampton Roads in Desert Storm- A Star Spangled Salute

Betty Francis and Jack Dorsey

(The Donning Company, 1991)

From Eros to Gaia

Freeman Dyson

(New York: Random House, 1992)

A Whole New Mind

Daniel Pink

(New York: Penguin Group, 2006)

Leaving Earth

Robert Zimmerman

(Washington, D.C., Joseph Henry Press, 2003)

A Study of History

Arnold Toynbee

(New York and London: Oxford University Press and Dell Publishing, 1965)

The Molecule of More

Daniel Z. Lieberman, M.D. and Michael E. Long

(Dallas, Texas: BenBella Books, 2018)

AFTERWORD

This book referred several times to brain structure. Understanding how to foster more right brain function is important for anyone who chooses a leadership lifestyle. This gives one a more global view of a problem/ issue and potential solutions. In addition, knowing how to develop a point of view based on an active imagination is critical. It is also important to recognize how the brain is structured in terms of its dopamine channels. Basically, there are two channels. One or the other is on all the time. The first is channel one. Its purpose it is to help us think in terms of the future and future possibilities. This is the 'want or desire' channel.

The second is channel two which regulates our emotional attachment to the present. It seeks to focus our attention and find joy in the present moment. While both are regulated by dopamine, they have exactly opposite effects on our behavior and outlook. We all have both channels. When we want more, and cannot wait for the next new thing, or the need to invent a better future we are tuned into the first channel. This is felt as a restlessness.

When we are happy, at peace, satisfied and able to focus on what is happening around us we are tuned into the second channel. Depending on the assessment of our current outlook on life we can tell which channel dominates most of our life. For the

Afterword

leadership lifestyle it is important to find a balance between the two so we can be competent, successful, and happy. Too much time on either channel makes us unbalanced and not capable of being an effective leader or human being.

What can you do? Look at your calendar. If you are spending too much time on channel one activities you can look toward meditation, yoga or others that take you offline and look within. If you are too introspective and spend most of your time on channel two you can set some goals, write out some plans and calendar some action steps to move forward.

All of this is easy to achieve with a little discipline and the setting of new habits. It begins with awareness of your current preferred channel of activity. This is similar to the wisdom offered by the Yin and Yang symbol addressed earlier on the book. Yang is activity in the world and Yin is the introspective activity of our mind and spirit.

As suggested in an earlier chapter to find and operate from a balanced 'middle way' is important. This allows you to think, act and express yourself effectively in the world. The middle way was the one preferred by the sages of antiquity. Aristotle, Buddha, and Confucius, (AKA: The ABC's) all stood by the wisdom of the middle way. You will always end up out of balance from time to time, but it is an easy matter to self-assess and get back on course.

If you follow the outline provided on how to build a Personal Lifestyle Leadership Map you will create a balanced approach. Then the goal is to implement and maintain it. This is a critical activity for anyone who has chosen to live the life of a leader.

www.ingramcontent.com/pod-product-compliance
Lightning Source LLC
Chambersburg PA
CBHW052318220526
45472CB00001B/176